Celebrity Snapper!

Taking the Ultimate Celebrity Photo

Susie Hodge

A & C Black • London

Produced for A&C Black by
 Monkey Puzzle Media Ltd
The Rectory, Eyke, Woodbridge,
Suffolk IP12 2QW, UK

Published by A&C Black Publishers Limited
38 Soho Square, London W1D 3HB

First published 2008

ISBN 978-1-4081-0023-3 (hardback)
ISBN 978-1-4081-0095-0 (paperback)

A CIP catalogue record for this book is available
from the British Library.

Editor: Polly Goodman
Design: Mayer Media Ltd
Picture research: Lynda Lines
Series consultant: Jane Turner

This book is produced using paper that is made
from wood grown in managed, sustainable forests.
It is natural, renewable and recyclable. The logging
and manufacturing processes conform to the
environmental regulations of the country of origin.

Printed in China by C & C Offset Printing Co., Ltd

Picture acknowledgements
Corbis pp. 5 (Patrick Giardino), 6 (Sunset
Boulevard), 7 (Hulton-Deutsch Collection), 11
(David Pu'u), 15 (Mario Anzuoni/Reuters), 18
(Dusko Despotovic), 19 (David Koskas), 20 (Lucas
Jackson/Reuters), 22 (Alessia Pierdomenico/Reuters);
Getty Images pp. 1, 4, 9 (Ryan McVay), 13, 14,
24 (James Devaney), 25, 28; iStockphoto pp. 8 top,
8 bottom left; MPM Images pp. 8 bottom left, 10;
Reuters p. 23 (Kiyoshi Ota); Rex Features pp. 12
(Julian Makey), 16 (Dave Lewis), 17 (Mr JCY);
Richard Young Photography pp. 26, 27; Topfoto
pp. 21 both (National Pictures), 29 (PA).

The front cover shows a paparrazzi photographer
with a "Map to the Stars' Homes" in Los Angeles,
USA (Corbis/Richard Ransier).

Every effort has been made to contact copyright
holders of material reproduced in this book. Any
omissions will be rectified in subsequent printings if
notice is given to the publishers.

CONTENTS

Abbreviations   **m** stands for metres   •   **ft** stands for feet   •   **in** stands for inches   •
km stands for kilometres

Who are the paparazzi?

People love finding out what celebrities are up to. That creates lots of work for extreme photographers, called the paparazzi.

Paparazzi are photographers who are constantly on the hunt for celebrities and public figures. The best paparazzi photos can be sold for hundreds of thousands of dollars. Those prices mean it's very competitive, and "paps" take more and more risks to get a front-page picture.

The actress Portia de Rossi arrives at the Oscars in Hollywood, in February 2007. Most celebrities like being photographed when they're looking their best!

La Dolce Vita

The word *paparazzi* comes from a film called *La Dolce Vita*, which was made in 1960. In it, there was a celebrity photographer called Paparazzo.

celebrities people who are famous

4

How do paparazzi get their shots?

What are the tricks of the trade?

What kind of equipment do they use?

paparazzi photographers who take photographs of celebrities

The first paps

When **portrait photography** was invented in the 1840s, people rushed to have their photos taken. Many people believed that, unlike painting, photography was a science that revealed the truth.

Photographers knew, however, that they could bend the truth in the way they took photos. Early photographs of famous figures were carefully planned, just like paintings. It wasn't until the mid-20th century that photographers snapped pictures without setting them up first.

*From the 1840s to the 1950s, most celebrity portrait photos were dramatic and carefully planned. They were often **retouched** by hand with paint after the photo was printed, to please the sitter.*

Flattering photos

To make a celebrity look softer in a photo, sometimes Vaseline™ was smeared on the camera lens. To make the photo sharp and dramatic, a light was reflected off a shiny surface to light up the face.

portrait photography   the photography of individual people

For early photos, any movement would ruin the picture. No wonder people rarely smiled for the photographer!

Metal clamp held the head still.

Person had to sit rigidly still for up to 30 minutes.

retouched   when a photograph is improved or changed by adding details or removing faults

Lights, camera, action!

Just think, every time you see something, your eyes are taking a picture, like a camera constantly at work.

Cameras work just like human eyes. They both have a **lens** that focuses light through a small hole. Light travels from the subject of a photo through the camera lens and is recorded as an image on a **sensor**. This is the same as light travelling through the eye to the **retina**.

Object

Sensor

Lens

Retina

LIGHT

LIGHT

Eye

Light travels in straight lines. It travels through the lens of a camera or eye and is recorded as an image.

Taking a photo

To take a photo, you press a button on the camera to open the **shutter**, which lets light into the camera. The amount of time the shutter is open controls how much light reaches the sensor.

lens part of a camera or eye that focuses an image

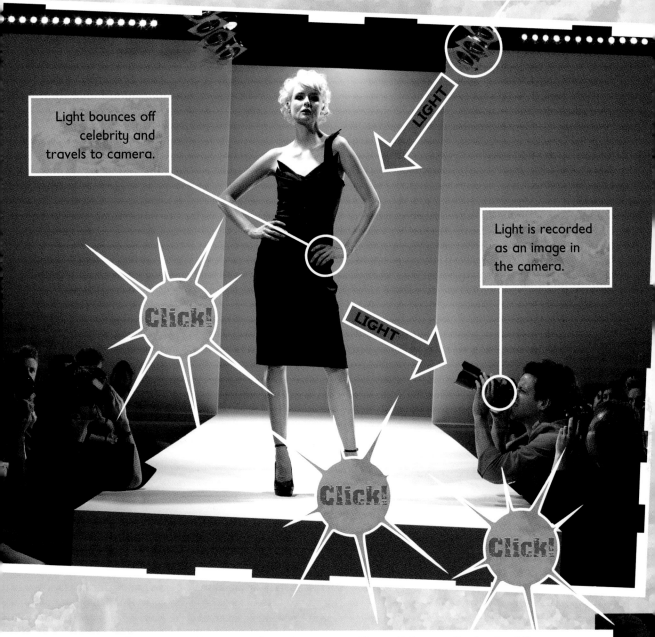

Photographers take photos of a model on a catwalk.

Stage lights point at catwalk.

Light bounces off celebrity and travels to camera.

LIGHT

Light is recorded as an image in the camera.

LIGHT

Click!

Click!

Click!

sensor   part of a camera that records an image   **retina**   lining on the back of the eye

Colour and light

You might think that there are hundreds of different colours, but all the different shades that you see are blended together out of just seven basic colours – the colours that make up white light.

The seven colours in light were first identified in 1666. A scientist called Isaac Newton discovered that if you shine light through a **prism**, it separates out into the colours of the **spectrum**: red, orange, yellow, green, blue, indigo and violet.

You can see the coloured dots of ink in this close-up of a colour print.

Colour printing

Although light is made up of seven colours, photos are printed using just three coloured inks – cyan, magenta, yellow – plus black. Tiny dots of ink are used rather than solid blocks of colour. The amount of dots that are used create different shades.

prism   a glass pyramid that splits white light into the colours of the spectrum

Tiny droplets of water vapour in the air work like prisms. They can separate light into the colours of the spectrum, creating a rainbow.

ORANGE
YELLOW
GREEN
INDIGO
VIOLET

White light contains all the colours of the spectrum blended together.

In a rainbow, the colours of white light are separated out.

spectrum   the seven colours in a rainbow, which make up white light

Flash power

Much of the paparazzi's work takes place at night, as celebrities leave nightclubs, restaurants or hotels. Fortunately for the paps, there are ways of taking photos even on the darkest of nights.

Unlike our eyes, cameras don't automatically adjust to changes in light. At night, there is not enough natural light to get a clear picture, so photographers make their own light using **flash**. Electronic flashes send out a short burst of bright light, which lights up the **subject** for a moment.

Camera flashes make the subject bright but the background dark, so the subject shows up more.

flash   a small, bright lamp that gives a quick burst of light to take a photograph

Fast!
Light travels at about 300,000 km (186,000 miles) per second.

Flash!
Camera flash travels to the face in a split second.

LIGHT

LIGHT

Bounce!
Light bounces off face and travels back to the camera.

Singer Jay Kay is caught in a paparazzo's camera flash as he is bundled into a car by security men.

subject in photography, the object that is being photographed

Exposed!

When paparazzi want to take photos at night without being spotted or given away by their flash, they increase the exposure on their cameras.

The exposure is the amount of light that gets into a camera. It is controlled by the **aperture** and shutter speed. The aperture is how wide the shutter opens. In dim light, it can be made wider to let in more light. The shutter speed is the length of time the shutter stays open. In dim light, it is made slower to let in more light.

In dark conditions, the aperture is wide and the shutter speed is slow. The shutter should be kept open for between 3 and 30 seconds.

The photographer increased the exposure for this photograph to let enough light into the camera.

aperture   the opening in a lens that lets light into a camera

14

In lighter conditions, the aperture can be narrower and the shutter speed faster – between 1 and 3 seconds.

exposure   the amount of light that can get into a camera

The hunt and chase

Celebrity snappers go to great lengths to find celebrities. They work like private detectives, paying contacts to let them know when their targets might appear. Then they use extreme tactics to get to them.

Some paparazzi perch in trees or on rooftops. Others rent helicopters or boats to photograph private events. Some even disguise themselves as waiters, policemen or cleaners to catch celebrities unawares.

Living dangerously – a paparazzo hangs out of a helicopter with his camera hundreds of metres up in the air.

Dangerous tactics

Snatching photos of people who don't want to be photographed started in the 1930s. It might look exciting, but paparazzi tactics can be deadly dangerous. Princess Diana died following a high-speed chase involving the paparazzi in 1997.

contacts people who have useful connections to celebrities or events

These two photographers climbed up 5 m (15 ft) of scaffolding to take photos of a celebrity in a hotel room across the street.

Celebrity in hotel room across the street.

Paparazzi hide in scaffolding. They'll wait there for hours if necessary, just for one shot.

They cut holes in the netting to get a clear shot.

Long-distance photos

When celebrities are holidaying on remote beaches or distant private yachts, it is sometimes impossible to get close up. So the paparazzi have to take photos from a distance.

When celebrities don't notice the photographer, they are more likely to act naturally.

To take photos of celebrities from far away, the paparazzi use cameras with **telephoto** and **zoom lenses**. These lenses can take pictures of objects up to 48 kilometres (30 miles) away. Celebrities caught by telephoto lenses are often completely unaware that they are being photographed.

No privacy

Many celebrities get very angry when they are photographed secretly because they feel they don't have any privacy. In 2005, Angelina Jolie was upset when she was shown photos of herself on holiday in Africa with Brad Pitt. The pictures had been taken from about 10 kilometres (6 miles) away.

telephoto lenses   lenses on a camera that make an image appear larger

Telephoto lens

Celebrity on beach

Paparazzi hide behind rocks.

zoom lenses lenses on a camera that make an image larger or smaller

Zooming in

Photographers use a variety of zoom and telephoto lenses at a top fashion show in New York City.

So how do telephoto and zoom lenses work? Both lenses can magnify everything, making the subject seem bigger.

A telephoto lens is a long lens that makes distant objects look bigger. This creates a photo that is similar to moving closer to the object. A zoom lens can make the subject bigger or smaller.

magnify to make larger

Telephoto lenses make distant objects appear **bigger.**

Some lenses make the pictures sharper.

Micro-cameras

You hear a click that sounds just like a camera, but there's no camera in sight ... you've probably been snapped by a micro-camera!

New technology has developed cameras so tiny that they now fit inside mobile phones, portable media players, and even tie clips and pens. This means there are even more ways of taking celebrity snaps, and if you're in the right place at the right time, you could become a celebrity snapper, too!

A video camera is hidden in this pen!

Handkerchief snaps

In the mid-20th century, photographer Henri Cartier-Bresson sometimes wrapped a large handkerchief around his camera and would pretend to blow his nose while he took photos.

Video camera

Digital camera

Phone camera

Fans use all sorts of cameras to take photos of their favourite celebrities.

Red-carpet photography

At film premieres, award ceremonies and celebrity parties, a different type of photographer snaps away at the side of the red carpet – these are event photographers, not paparazzi – and their job is quite different.

Celebrities know they will be captured on camera at events, and often the photos will help to **promote** a new book, song or film. The celebrities usually turn up looking good and work with the photographers to make the best photos possible.

Some celebrities, like Paris Hilton, encourage photographers' attention. But if celebrities are photographed too often, their pictures become less valuable.

promote   to encourage the sale of something

On the red carpet, photographers compete with each other to get the best shots.

Photographers ask celebrities to stand in the spot with the best light.

Snap!

Click!

Celebrities often **pose** for the photographers to make the photo more interesting.

pose in photography, to take a special position or expression for a photograph

Before and after

In magazines and advertisements, people often look perfect. Many photos of celebrities or models are retouched before they are printed.

There are many tricks that can be used on a photo to achieve the perfect look. Computer programmes can smooth skin, lighten shadows under the eyes, and remove blemishes and wrinkles. Teeth can be straightened, hair colour changed, eyebrows raised and eye shapes altered.

Before ...

Photo editing

Photographers often adjust, or **edit** their photos using computer programmes before sending them to magazines. They can make the subject look more focused and make images sharper. This is called photo editing.

edit   to prepare something for printing

Hair made darker.

Skin colour changed.

Eyes made brighter and clearer.

Nose made smaller.

Wrinkles removed.

Jaw made smaller.

Blemishes removed.

Lips made redder.

... and after. Most models don't look as good in real life as they do in magazines!

The need for speed

How do you take a photo of a sporting celebrity whizzing past you at over 160 kilometres (100 miles) per hour?

At this motor-racing pit stop, the fast action has been caught on camera and made to look blurred and distorted.

Photographers have two main ways of taking fast-action photos. They either "freeze" the action, making the subject sharp but leaving the background a blur, or they make the movement look blurred.

• For sharp action shots, photographers use fast shutter speeds.
• For blurred action shots, photographers use slower shutter speeds.

focus to point the lens of a camera at the subject and adjust the lens to get a clear picture

Capturing speed

To catch fast-moving subjects:
- **Focus** on your target.
- Stand in the best position.
- **Pan** ahead of the subject with your camera.
- Take several shots quickly.

Blurry background

Crystal-clear
subject

When photographers pan (move) their cameras to keep up with a moving subject, the subject appears to stay in place while other features stretch into streaks. This shows movement really well.

pan   to move the camera while taking the photo

Glossary

aperture the opening in a lens that lets light into a camera

celebrities people who are famous

contacts people who have useful connections to celebrities or events

edit to prepare something for printing

exposure the amount of light that can get into a camera

flash a small, bright lamp that gives a quick burst of light to take a photograph

focus to point the lens of a camera at the subject and adjust the lens to get a clear picture

lens part of a camera or eye that focuses an image

magnify to make larger

pan to move the camera while taking the photo

paparazzi (singular: paparazzo) photographers who take photographs of celebrities

portrait photography the photography of individual people

pose in photography, to take a special position or expression for a photograph

prism a glass pyramid that splits white light into the colours of the spectrum

promote to encourage the sale of something

retina lining on the back of the eye

retouched when a photograph is improved or changed by adding details or removing faults

sensor part of a camera that records an image

shutter part of a camera that opens and closes to let in light

spectrum the seven colours in a rainbow, which make up white light

subject in photography, the object that is being photographed

telephoto lenses lenses on a camera that make an image appear larger

zoom lenses lenses on a camera that make an image larger or smaller

Further information

Books

Digital Photo Madness!: 50 Weird and Wacky Things to Do with Your Digital Camera by Thom Gaines (Lark Books, 2006)

Essential Science: Light and Seeing by Peter Riley (Watts, 2006)
Essential facts about light and sight with experiments.

How Does Science Work? Light by Carol Ballard (Hodder Wayland, 2006)
The science of light explained in clear and simple text.

The Kids' Guide to Digital Photography: How to Shoot, Save, Play With and Print Your Digital Photos by Jenni Bidner (Lark Books, 2004)

Paparazzi by Peter Howe (Artisan, 2005)
A big glossy book with photographs and stories by paparazzi.

Science Answers: Light by Chris Cooper (Heinemann, 2003)
Aspects of the science of light linked to everyday examples, including experiments.

Science in Your Life, Light: Look Out! by Wendy Sadler (Raintree, 2005)
An introduction to the science of light applied to everyday life.

Science Investigations: Light by John Gorman (Hodder Wayland, 2006)
A question-and-answer approach to the science of light.

Voyage of a Light Beam: Light Energy by Andrew Solway (Raintree, 2005)
An introduction to the science of light.

Websites

www.vam.ac.uk/collections/photography/index.html
The Victoria and Albert Museum's Photography gallery, with photographs acquired since 1852.

http://photo.net/learn/portraits/
How to take interesting portraits of friends and family with simple equipment.

www.learner.org/teacherslab/science/light/
A website for young people including a page with hands-on activities for teachers and their students about the science of light, including light, colour, reflection and refraction.

Index